MINECRAFT

© MOJANG

Written by Stephanie Milton, with help from Paul Soares Jr, FyreUK, and CNB Minecraft
Designed by Andrea Philpots and Joe Bolder
Illustrations by Theo Cordner, Joe Bolder, and FyreUK
Production by Louis Harvey and Caroline Hancock
Special thanks to Lydia Winters, Owen Hill, and Junkboy

&MOJANG

Published by arrangement with Mojang and Egmont®.

ISBN 978-0-545-82323-4

14 13 12 11 10 9 8 7 6 5   16 17 18 19 20/0

Printed in China   62
First published 2014
This edition first printing 2015

MINECRAFT

MOJANG

COMBAT HANDBOOK

CONTENTS

InTRODUCTION

WELCOME TO THE OFFICIAL MINECRAFT COMBAT HANDBOOK. IT'S ESSENTIAL READING FOR WARRIORS!

This book is packed with tips from Minecraft experts like master builders FyreUK, YouTube sensation Paul Soares Jr., and redstone expert CNB Minecraft.

Read on to learn how to defend your home, build a fort, fight hostile monsters, set cunning traps, thrive in PVP (player versus player) mode, evade death in the Nether, and battle the dreaded Ender Dragon in the mysterious End dimension.

With the help of this handbook, you'll be a Minecraft warrior of the highest order in no time!

TIP: STAYING SAFE ONLINE

Playing Minecraft on multiplayer servers is a lot of fun! Here are a few simple rules to help you stay safe and keep the world of Minecraft a great place to spend time:

- Never give out your real name — don't use it as your username.
- Never give out any of your personal details.
- Never tell anybody which school you go to or how old you are.
- Never tell anybody your password except a parent or guardian.

Weapons are items used to deal damage to other players or mobs, or to block attacks. There are several basic weapons that should be at the core of any warrior's arsenal.

SWORD

A sword's sharpness makes it the best weapon to use during close-range/melee combat. A sword can be crafted from 1 stick plus 2 pieces of wood, cobblestone, smelted iron, smelted gold, or diamond gems.

Diamond swords are by far the most durable and will inflict the most damage, but diamond is one of the trickiest elements to find in Minecraft because it generates deep underground. If you don't have any diamonds, just craft a sword out of the strongest element you have on hand.

SWORD DURABILITY TABLE

MATERIAL	Wood	Stone	Iron	Gold	Diamond
DURABILITY	60	132	251	33	1562
DAMAGE ♥	5	6	7	5	8
APPROX KILLS	15–24	39–66	87–138	8–13	624–1015
LIFETIME DAMAGE ♥	150–240	396–660	878–1380	82–132	6,248–10,153

WOODEN SWORD RECIPE

A great starter weapon, but you'll soon need a more powerful upgrade.

COBBLESTONE SWORD RECIPE

Has a little more bite and will work until you can access rare ores.

IRON SWORD RECIPE

Now we're talking! An iron sword will last a while.

GOLDEN SWORD RECIPE

A golden sword isn't very durable, but it's the easiest to enchant.

DIAMOND SWORD RECIPE

The ultimate fighting implement for the player who intends to dominate.

SWORD MAINTENANCE

You can rename and repair a sword on an anvil. Access your anvil and place the sword in the first slot, then either add a second sword to repair or change the text to rename. The cost in experience points will appear at the bottom.

ANVIL RECIPE

An anvil can be crafted from 3 iron blocks (crafted from 9 iron ingots), and another 4 iron ingots.

REPAIR & NAME

Sword of Doom_

Enchantment Cost: 7

... CONTINUED

BOW AND ARROWS

The main advantage of a bow and arrows is that, unlike a sword, you can use it from a distance and keep out of range of your enemy's attack.

BOW RECIPE

A bow can be crafted from 3 sticks and 3 pieces of string (dropped by spiders when they die).

Durability: 385

ARROWS RECIPE

Arrows can be crafted from flint (obtained by mining gravel), a stick, and a feather (dropped by chickens when they die).

A fully charged bow and arrows can deal 9 points of damage per hit. To charge your bow, just hold down the Use Item button until it begins to shake. This will make the arrows go farther and do maximum damage. It takes just 1 second to fully charge, which is very useful when you're in a fight.

DID YOU KNOW?

You can enchant a bow with a variety of helpful effects such as unbreaking, punch, and flame. Turn to pages 48–53 for more information on enchanting.

ENCHANT

	6
	8
	30

DISPENSERS

As its name suggests, a dispenser is a mechanism that stores and dispenses items. It can be used to fire arrows, eggs, snowballs, and splash potions at your opponents, and it can hold up to 9 stacks of 64 items.

DISPENSER RECIPE

A dispenser can be crafted from 7 blocks of cobblestone, redstone dust, and a bow.

LEVER RECIPE

Now connect it to a lever using redstone dust. A lever can be crafted from 1 cobblestone and a stick.

Access the dispenser then drag the required items into the 9 item slots that appear. Now you're all set to start using your dispenser.

Pull the lever to activate the dispenser and your ammunition of choice will be fired out. Just make sure it's pointed in the right direction.

`'.. |·= Ш ..·"·"II`

. . . CONTINUED

FLINT AND STEEL

This is a handy tool that allows you to make fire and can be used as a weapon against your enemies. Once crafted, select it in your hotbar and use it on a flammable block to set it alight. Aim for the block underneath your opponent, or a block directly in their path, and you'll soon get rid of them.

FLINT AND STEEL RECIPE

Craft a flint and steel from flint (found when you mine gravel blocks), and an iron ingot.

LAVA BUCKET

A lava bucket can be used to damage several opponents at once, since it allows you to place lava in their path or to drop it on top of them. Find some lava, select the bucket from your hotbar, and use it on the lava to collect it. To place the lava, just use the bucket in the desired destination.

BUCKET RECIPE

You'll need 3 iron ingots to make a bucket in which to hold your lava.

 WARNING: You can easily set yourself or your surroundings on fire when using fire or lava. Keep a water bucket in your hotbar so you always have it handy to put out any accidental fires.

TNT

Activate the TNT using a flint and steel, fire, a redstone current, or another explosion in the near vicinity. If lighting with a flint and steel, make sure you get away quickly, or else you'll go BOOM along with the TNT!

TNT RECIPE

Craft a block of TNT from 5 gunpowder (dropped by creepers when they die) and 4 blocks of sand.

TNT: a simple yet effective way to annihilate an enemy base.

ARMOR

Minecraft warriors need armor to protect themselves from attack and damage, especially when battling other players. A full set consists of a helmet, chest plate, trousers, and boots.

There are 5 types of armor: leather, gold, chain mail, iron, and diamond. Leather is the weakest, and diamond the strongest.

Leather · Gold · Chain mail · Iron · Diamond

You can craft armor from leather, gold ingots, iron ingots, or diamond. You will need to make each individual piece from units of the same material.

HELMET RECIPE

Craft a helmet from 5 units of your chosen material.

CHEST PLATE RECIPE

A chest plate can be crafted from 8 units.

TROUSERS RECIPE

Trousers can be crafted from 7 units.

BOOTS RECIPE

Craft a pair of boots from 4 units.

Chain-mail armor cannot be crafted, but can sometimes be acquired through villager trading, or if a mob drops it when it dies. Leather, gold, iron, and diamond armor can also be dropped by mobs.

Once your armor is crafted, simply place each piece in the corresponding armor slot in your inventory, and it will appear on your body.

PROTECTION

Armor will protect you from the following forms of damage:

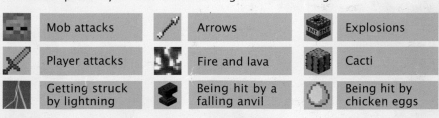

	Mob attacks		Arrows		Explosions
	Player attacks		Fire and lava		Cacti
	Getting struck by lightning		Being hit by a falling anvil		Being hit by chicken eggs

Armor will not protect you from the following forms of damage, but these forms won't reduce the armor's durability, either:

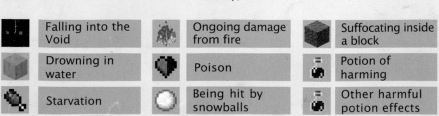

	Falling into the Void		Ongoing damage from fire		Suffocating inside a block
	Drowning in water		Poison		Potion of harming
	Starvation		Being hit by snowballs		Other harmful potion effects

ARMOR ...CONTINUED

DEFENSE POINTS

As soon as you equip your armor in your inventory, an armor bar will pop up above your hotbar. It consists of 10 chest plates.

Each chest plate is worth 2 defense points and represents 8% protection. So, the total protection you can achieve with armor is 80% — sadly, you'll never be completely immune to damage in Survival mode.

The more defense points your armor has, the more damage it will absorb over its lifetime. For example, a complete set of diamond armor will protect you from 80% of damage, compared to a complete set of iron armor, which will protect you from only 60%, or leather, which is only 28%.

DEFENSE POINTS TABLE

TYPE	FULL SET OF ARMOR	HELMET	CHEST	LEGS	BOOTS
Leather	🛡🛡🛡🛡	🛡	🛡🛡	🛡	🛡
Gold	🛡🛡🛡🛡🛡	🛡	🛡🛡🛡	🛡🛡	🛡
Chain	🛡🛡🛡🛡🛡	🛡	🛡🛡🛡	🛡🛡	🛡
Iron	🛡🛡🛡🛡🛡🛡	🛡	🛡🛡🛡	🛡🛡🛡	🛡
Diamond	🛡🛡🛡🛡🛡🛡🛡🛡	🛡🛡	🛡🛡🛡🛡	🛡🛡🛡	🛡🛡

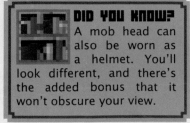

DID YOU KNOW?
A mob head can also be worn as a helmet. You'll look different, and there's the added bonus that it won't obscure your view.

ARMOR STANDS

You can display your armor on an armor stand when it's not in use. This will save you valuable space in your inventory, and it can make an interesting decoration for your house, too. Once crafted, simply interact with the stand while holding your armor and it will appear on the stand.

ARMOR STAND RECIPE

An armor stand can be crafted from 6 sticks and a stone slab.

 You can dye leather armor by crafting it with a dye of your choice. Just add the item of armor to your crafting area along with the dye to combine the two.

 TIP: It's a good idea to keep a spare set of armor in your inventory, especially if you're playing in PVP mode. That way, if your current armor is destroyed, you can quickly replace it and get back into battle.

MOB COMBAT

Fighting hostile monsters is the best way to outfit yourself with supplies for future combat. Let's start with the Overworld mobs before venturing to the Nether and the End.

SILVERFISH

HEALTH POINTS: 8 ♥♥♥♥

ATTACK STRENGTH: 1 ♥

ATTACK METHOD: Will run or jump toward you and inflict damage by touching you and by pushing you around. When 1 silverfish is attacked, more may awaken nearby and you may easily find yourself swarmed.

SPAWNS: From monster egg blocks and monster spawners found in strongholds. Rarely, underground in extreme hills biomes when a monster egg block is broken.

VULNERABLE TO: Lava, gravel

DO	DON'T
Try building a 2-block-tall column to stand on and attack the silverfish safely from above.	Use splash potions. This will result in you being swarmed by silverfish.

SPIDER

HEALTH POINTS: 16 ♥♥♥♥♥♥♥♥

ATTACK STRENGTH: 2-3 ♥ - ♥♥

ATTACK METHOD: Will leap toward you and hit you, inflicting damage until you die. Only hostile in low light levels. Once hostile they will remain so, even in daylight.

SPAWNS: In the Overworld in light levels of 7 or less.

VULNERABLE TO:

Lava, cacti, TNT, fire, falling

USEFUL DROPS:

0-2 string, which can be used to make a bow.

0-1 spider eyes, which can be used in potions.

DO

Try to get to higher ground than the spider. This will allow you to attack it repeatedly, preventing it from jumping up to your level.

DON'T

Let the spider have the high ground. This will give the spider the perfect opportunity to pounce on you from above.

CAVE SPIDER

HEALTH POINTS: 12 ♥♥♥♥♥♥

ATTACK STRENGTH: 1 ♥

ATTACK METHOD: Will leap toward you and bite you, inflicting their venom.

SPAWNS: From monster spawners in abandoned mineshafts.

VULNERABLE TO:

Lava, cacti, TNT, fire, falling

USEFUL DROPS:

0-2 string, which can be used to make a bow.
0-1 spider eyes, which can be used in potions.

DO

Go straight for the source of the problem: Try to find the cave spider spawner and disable it with lava.

DON'T

Forget that, unlike regular spiders, cave spiders can fit through spaces 1 block wide and half a block tall.

SLIME

HEALTH POINTS: Large: 16 ♥♥♥♥♥♥♥♥ Medium:4 ♥♥
Tiny: 1 ♥

ATTACK STRENGTH: Large: 4 ♥♥ Medium: 2♥ Tiny: 0

ATTACK METHOD: Will hop toward you and bump into you repeatedly, inflicting damage until you die.

SPAWNS: Below level 40 in specific chunks, at any light level. In swamp biomes between levels 50 and 70, in light levels of 7 or less.

VULNERABLE TO:

Lava, cacti, TNT, fire, falling

USEFUL DROPS: ◯

Tiny slime drop 0–2 slimeballs, which can be used to make magma cream for potions.

DO

Try forcing the slimes into a nearby lava pool or lake. If you manage to keep them submerged, they'll quickly catch fire and die.

DON'T

Get yourself cornered by a swarm of slimes in a cave. They will soon deal enough damage to overpower you in a restricted space.

CREEPER

HEALTH POINTS: 20 ♥♥♥♥♥♥♥♥♥♥

ATTACK STRENGTH: 49 (regular) ♥ ✕ 24.5 and 97 (charged) ♥ ✕ 48.5

ATTACK METHOD: Runs at you and explodes in your face.

SPAWNS: In the Overworld in areas with a light level of 7 or less, but not on transparent blocks like glass. They don't die when the sun rises.

VULNERABLE TO:

Lava, cacti, TNT, fire, falling, durable weapons, bow and arrows

WHO TO TAKE:

Cats and ocelots. They wouldn't hurt a fly, but will send creepers running for the hills.

USEFUL DROPS:

Creepers drop 0-2 pieces of gunpowder, which you can use to make TNT and fire charges.

DO	DON'T

Keep a safe distance to stay out of range of their explosion. Always attack with a bow and arrows before resorting to melee weapons.	Get too close, especially if you hear a hissing sound. Try to avoid close-quarters combat, or you may be blown to pieces.

SKELETON

HEALTH POINTS: 20 ♥♥♥♥♥♥♥♥♥♥

ATTACK STRENGTH: 1-5 ♥ - ♥♥♥

ATTACK METHOD: Will shoot at you with a bow and arrows.

SPAWNS: In the Overworld in areas with a light level of 7 or less, but not on transparent blocks like glass or half blocks.

VULNERABLE TO:

Lava, cacti, TNT, fire, falling, daylight, splash potion of healing

USEFUL DROPS:

0-2 arrows, their bow (rarely — may be enchanted), random armor (rarely, if equipped — may be enchanted).

DO	DON'T

Use its own weapon against it and shoot it from a distance with a bow and arrows.	Let it pick up any headgear. If it manages to grab a helmet or pumpkin it will become immune to sunlight.

ZOMBIE

HEALTH POINTS: 20 ❤❤❤❤❤❤❤❤❤❤

ATTACK STRENGTH: 2-4 ❤ - ❤❤

ATTACK METHOD: Will amble toward you and touch you to inflict damage until you die.

SPAWNS: In the Overworld in areas with a light level of 7 or less, but not on transparent blocks like glass.

VULNERABLE TO:

Lava, cacti, TNT, fire, falling, daylight, splash potion of healing

USEFUL DROPS:

Iron sword and random armor (rarely, if equipped), which can come in handy if you're short on supplies.

DO

Try to lure them out into the sunshine if they're still hanging around in the shade when day comes. They won't last long!

DON'T

Get stuck in a long corridor. And don't let a zombie pick up any headgear, as this will prevent it from catching fire in the sunlight.

ZOMBIE VILLAGER

Five percent of zombies will be zombie villagers. You can tell them apart from regular zombies because their faces look like villager faces and have the distinctive long noses. They may spawn as a result of zombies attacking villagers.

DID YOU KNOW?

A zombie villager can be cured by throwing a splash potion of weakness at it and feeding it a golden apple.

BABY ZOMBIE

Another five percent of naturally spawned zombies will be baby zombies, and they spawn when a zombie kills a baby villager. Tiny though they may be, they're much faster than regular zombies and can fit through single-block gaps. They don't catch fire in sunlight, can deal as much damage as a regular zombie, and have the same number of health points as a regular zombie. So, to sum up, they are much trickier to deal with.

And, to make matters worse, they may also spawn wearing armor and can ride chickens. Yikes!

WITCH

HEALTH POINTS: 26 ♥♥♥♥♥♥♥♥♥♥♥♥♥

ATTACK METHOD: Will repeatedly throw splash potions of poison, weakness, harming, and slowness at you.

SPAWNS: In dimly lit areas, often in witch huts in swampland.

VULNERABLE TO:

Splash potion of poison and instant damage (but they are 85% immune to these), arrows

USEFUL DROPS:

0-6 gunpowder, which can be used to make TNT; 0-6 spider eyes, which can be used in potions (rarely).

DO

Use a bow and arrows to take a witch out, since the bow's range is farther than the witch's splash potion range.

DON'T

Set a witch alight with lava or fire as they will just drink a potion of fire resistance.

ENDERMAN

HEALTH POINTS: 40 ♥♥♥♥♥♥♥♥♥♥ ♥♥♥♥♥♥♥♥♥♥

ATTACK STRENGTH: 4-10 ♥♥ - ♥♥♥

ATTACK METHOD: Will teleport toward you and hit you, inflicting damage until you die.

SPAWNS: In the Overworld in areas with a light level of 7 or less, and in large numbers in the End.

VULNERABLE TO:

Lava, cacti, TNT, fire, falling, water

USEFUL DROPS:

0-1 ender pearls (needed to get to the End).

DO

Run for the nearest body of water or lava and get your back up against a wall to stop them teleporting behind you. If endermen take damage from either water or lava, they will return to a neutral state.

DON'T

Look directly at an enderman from the upper legs upward — this will be taken as a sign of hostility.

GUARDIAN

HEALTH POINTS: 30 ❤❤❤❤❤❤❤❤❤❤❤❤❤❤❤

ATTACK STRENGTH: 4-9 ❤❤ - ❤❤❤❤❤

ATTACK METHOD: Will shoot a laser beam at you and extend their body spikes toward you, inflicting a small amount of damage.

SPAWNS: Underwater, in ocean monuments.

VULNERABLE TO:

Weapons

USEFUL DROPS:

Raw fish, prismarine crystals, prismarine shards

DO

Try using a fishing rod to pull the guardian out of the water onto land, then hit it repeatedly with a sword until it dies.

DON'T

Expect to kill a guardian using regular melee techniques; the water will slow your movement and the guardian will have the upper hand.

ELDER GUARDIAN

HEALTH POINTS: 80 ❤ ✕40

ATTACK STRENGTH: 5-12 ❤❤❤ – ❤❤❤❤❤❤

ATTACK METHOD: Inflicts Mining Fatigue III on players nearby to protect the treasure in the monument, sends out a laser beam like the guardians.

SPAWNS: Underwater, in ocean monuments.

VULNERABLE TO:

Weapons

USEFUL DROPS:

Raw fish, wet sponge, prismarine crystals, prismarine shards

DO

Remember to enchant your diamond equipment with respiration and depth strider to help you mine quickly and safely in the monument.

DON'T

Get too close to an elder guardian if you manage to corner it; they will hit you with their body spikes, inflicting damage.

ENDERMITE

HEALTH POINTS: 8 ♥♥♥♥

ATTACK STRENGTH: 2 ♥

ATTACK METHOD: Will run or jump toward you and inflict damage by touching you and pushing you around. When 1 endermite is attacked, more may appear nearby and you may easily find yourself swarmed.

SPAWNS: Occasionally when endermen teleport, or when a player throws an ender pearl.

VULNERABLE TO:

Drowning in water, suffocation by walking on soul sand

DO	DON'T

Try building a 2-block-tall column to stand on and attack the endermites safely from above.	Let yourself get swarmed. Endermites are much more difficult to deal with in large numbers.

UTILITY MOBS

Struggling to defend your lands from hostile monsters? There are 2 special mobs that you can craft yourself. They're known as utility mobs, and they'd be more than happy to help you out.

IRON GOLEM

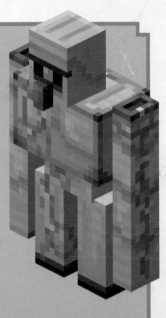

HEALTH POINTS: 100 ♥ ✕50

ATTACK STRENGTH: 7 – 21

♥♥♥♥ – ♥♥♥♥♥♥♥♥♥♥♥

ATTACK METHOD: Iron golems swing their arms around, hitting enemies and sending them flying to their deaths in one or two hits.

SPAWNS: When created by the player, or near groups of 10 villagers and 21 houses, in any light level.

VULNERABLE TO:

Lava, drowning, falling

USEFUL DROPS: 3–5 iron ingots, 0–2 poppies

HOW TO CRAFT: Place 4 solid blocks of iron (crafted from 9 iron ingots) in a T-shape, with a pumpkin or jack-o'-lantern on top.

SNOW GOLEM

HEALTH POINTS: 4 ♥♥

ATTACK METHOD: Will throw snowballs at enemy mobs. They don't harm anything except blazes and the Ender Dragon but can keep other mobs at bay by knocking them backward.

SPAWNS: When created by the player.

VULNERABLE TO:

Lava, water

USEFUL DROPS:

0-15 snowballs, which can be used as a weapon against blazes and the ender dragon.

HOW TO CRAFT: Stack 2 blocks of snow vertically, and place a pumpkin or jack-o'-lantern on top.

T..Mnalc Mub_

Fancy getting a loyal companion to follow you around and help scare away hostile mobs? There are 2 animals that can be tamed and made into pets for just such a purpose!

WOLF

Wolves can be tamed using bones. Once tame, they act like dogs, following you around and attacking hostile enemies.

VULNERABLE TO:

Lava, cacti, fire, falling, drowning, suffocation

OCELOT

Ocelots, found in jungle biomes, can be tamed using raw fish. Once tame, an ocelot will transform into 1 of 3 different breeds of cat and will scare creepers away from you. They're even immune to fall damage!

VULNERABLE TO:

Lava, cacti, fire, drowning, suffocation

CuMonT In THe NeTHer

The Nether is a hellish dimension, which you can access by creating a Nether portal in the Overworld. It's worth the trip, because you can pick up many useful items here that aren't available anywhere else.

You'll need a minimum of 10 blocks of obsidian to build a Nether portal. Once you've constructed the portal, use a flint and steel or a fire charge to activate it, and jump through the swirling portal blocks.

NETHER PORTAL

A full Nether portal can be crafted from 14 blocks of obsidian. If you're short on obsidian, save yourself 4 blocks and cut out the corners. It'll still work!

Before entering the Nether, equip yourself with the following:

 Enchanted armor

 Enchanted weapons

 Several stacks of cobblestone blocks to create safe paths and build a barrier to protect your Nether portal

 Flint and steel (you'll need this to relight your Nether portal if it's destroyed)

Torches Food

 DID YOU KNOW? In the PC/Mac Edition, 1 block in the Nether equals 8 blocks in the Overworld, so you can use the Nether as a shortcut to travel quickly across long distances. As long as you can handle the danger, that is! In the Console Edition the Nether is limited in size and 1 block equals 3 blocks in the Overworld. The Nether doesn't currently exist for the Pocket Edition.

GHAST

HEALTH POINTS: 10 ♥♥♥♥♥

ATTACK STRENGTH: 9–25
♥♥♥♥♥–♥♥♥♥♥♥♥♥♥♥♥♥♥

ATTACK METHOD: Will shoot fireballs out of their mouths.

SPAWNS: In the Nether, in a space of at least 5x4x5 blocks.

VULNERABLE TO:

Their own weapon. Give the ghast a taste of its own medicine and deflect those fireballs right back at them with one of your weapons.

USEFUL DROPS:

0–2 gunpowder, which can be used to make TNT; 0–1 ghast tears, which can be used in potions.

DO	DON'T

Try hooking a ghast with your fishing rod and drawing it in toward you so you can finish it off with a sword.	Underestimate the range of a ghast fireball. You'll be surprised by how far they can travel.

MAGMA CUBE

HEALTH POINTS: Large: 16 ❤❤❤❤❤❤❤❤ Medium:4 ❤❤
Tiny: 1 ❤

ATTACK STRENGTH: Large: 6 ❤❤❤ Medium: 4 ❤❤ Tiny: 3 ❤❤❤

ATTACK METHOD: Will hop toward you and bump into you, inflicting damage until you die.

SPAWNS: In the Nether.

VULNERABLE TO:

Durable weapons

USEFUL DROPS:

Large and medium magma cubes drop
0–1 magma cream, which can be used in potions.

DO

Try to hit them while they're in the air. That way you might be able to knock them backward over a ledge.

DON'T

Let a magma cube jump on top of you — you'll be surprised by how far they can travel and the damage they can do.

BLAZE

HEALTH POINTS: 20 ♥♥♥♥♥♥♥♥♥♥

ATTACK STRENGTH: 4-9 ♥♥- ♥♥♥♥♥

ATTACK METHOD: Will launch fireballs at you, or set itself on fire if close to you.

SPAWNS: In Nether fortresses.

VULNERABLE TO:

Snowballs, water

USEFUL DROPS:

0-1 blaze rods, which can be used in potions.

DO

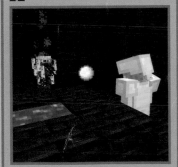

Drink a potion of fire resistance to protect yourself, since all their attack methods involve fire. Once face-to-face with a blaze, use snowballs to weaken it, then finish it off with your sword.

DON'T

Try to take them on with just a sword. Blazes can fly and deal damage from a distance, so they'll soon kill you if you try melee combat.

WITHER SKELETON

HEALTH POINTS: 20 ♥♥♥♥♥♥♥♥♥♥

ATTACK STRENGTH: 4-10 ♥♥ - ♥♥♥♥♥

ATTACK METHOD: Will hit you with their sword, at which point you'll be afflicted with the wither effect for 10 seconds. You'll know this has happened, because your health bar will turn black and you'll be damaged over time due to its poison-like effect.

SPAWNS: Near Nether fortresses, in light levels of 7 or less.

VULNERABLE TO:

Diamond swords with the sharpness, smite, or looting enchantment

USEFUL DROPS:

Stone sword (rarely), wither skeleton skulls (rarely)

DO

Try to get yourself into a 2-block-tall space, as the wither skeleton won't be able to follow you. This way, you can attack and then move backward to avoid retaliation.

DON'T

Get too close. Wither skeletons rely on you being within range of their sword to attack you.

ZOMBIE PIGMAN

HEALTH POINTS: 20 ♥♥♥♥♥♥♥♥♥♥

ATTACK STRENGTH: 5–13
♥♥♥–♥♥♥♥♥♥♥

ATTACK METHOD: A zombie pigman is neutral until you attack. When provoked, it will hit you with its sword, inflicting damage until you die.

SPAWNS: In any 2-block-tall space in the Nether.

VULNERABLE TO:

Enchanted bow and arrows, durable weapons

USEFUL DROPS:

Golden sword (rarely — may be enchanted). Gold ingots (rarely), needed to craft gold armor and weapons.

DO	DON'T

Attack them from a distance, with an enchanted bow and arrows, and try to pick them off one by one.	Attack one if several more are in the area. They will all turn on you if you do, and you could find yourself swarmed.

WITHER

The wither is a boss mob like the Ender Dragon (see pages 44–47). It's player-made and can be crafted from 4 blocks of soul sand arranged in a T-shape, with 3 wither skeleton skulls on top. The last block you place must be a skull or the wither won't spawn.

HEALTH POINTS: 300 ❤ ✕150

ATTACK STRENGTH: 5–12 ❤❤❤ – ❤❤❤❤❤❤

ATTACK METHOD: Launches wither skulls, which will inflict the wither effect (a poison that can kill you) upon contact with players.

SPAWNS: In the Overworld, when a player creates one.

VULNERABLE TO: Potions, durable weapons

WEAPONS TO TAKE:

Enchanted diamond sword combined with splash potions and an enchanted bow

WHO TO TAKE: Snow golems will attack the wither and distract it. To craft one, simply place a pumpkin on top of 2 vertically stacked snow blocks (see page 32).

USEFUL DROPS: 1 Nether star, which can be used to make a beacon — a block that is both a strong light source and a source of power for players. If placed on a pyramid, it gives selected buffs to players within a certain radius.

STRATEGY: Preparation, preparation, preparation! Don't even think about spawning a wither until you're wearing armor and have the right weapons.

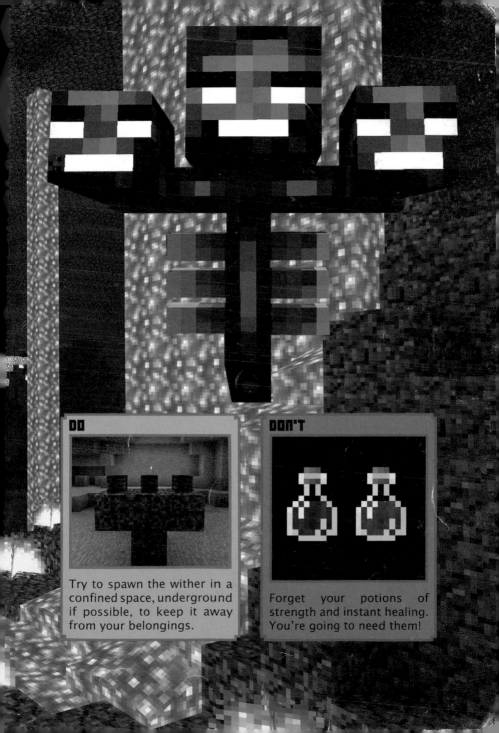

DO

Try to spawn the wither in a confined space, underground if possible, to keep it away from your belongings.

DON'T

Forget your potions of strength and instant healing. You're going to need them!

GETTING TO THE END

The End is a terrifying spit of land in the middle of a spacelike dimension known as the Void. It's almost completely barren, but is inhabited by endermen and the terrifying Ender Dragon.

If you can defeat the Ender Dragon you'll be rewarded handsomely, so it's well worth the trip. While you're there you can collect End stone, which has a high blast resistance. To get there you'll need to locate an End portal, found in portal rooms within strongholds. To find your nearest stronghold, you're likely to need several eyes of ender, and then up to 12 more to activate it.

EYE OF ENDER RECIPE

You'll need an ender pearl and blaze powder (made from blaze rods dropped by blazes in the Nether).

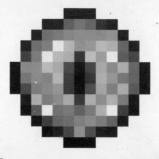

1

Use your eye of ender and it will fly away from you into the air before dropping back to the ground. Follow it, pick it up, and repeat. There's a 1 in 5 chance that the eye will shatter when it drops, which is why you need several.

2

Eventually the eye will keep falling onto the same spot of land. This is where you'll find the stronghold, and you'll need to dig underground to get in. Just remember the Number One Rule for Minecraft: Never dig straight down or you could fall into the lava in the center of the portal.

3

Find the End portal — a lava pool surrounded by End portal blocks. This may take you a while if it's a large stronghold. All 12 portal blocks will need to be activated with eyes of ender before it will work.

When the portal is activated, jump through the center and you'll find yourself in the End. Good luck!

THE ENDER DRAGON

Once you get to the End, be prepared for awesome adventure and some serious combat. The Ender Dragon is ferociously aggressive, and there's nowhere to hide . . .

It's pretty dark in the End, so you might not spot the dragon immediately. But don't worry — the fearsome snarls and glowing purple eyes will soon alert you to its location. Plus, it'll pounce as soon as it spots you.

HEALTH POINTS: 200 ❤×100

ATTACK STRENGTH: 6–15 ❤❤❤ – ❤❤❤❤❤❤❤❤

ATTACK METHOD: Will dive toward you and hit you, inflicting damage until you die.

SPAWNS: In the End.

VULNERABLE TO: Not much. The Ender Dragon is immune to lava, fire, water, and enchantments, and only takes damage from swords and arrows.

DROPS: TOP SECRET

TIP: Diamond armor will protect you from endermen as well as the dragon, and wearing a pumpkin head stops endermen from attacking if you look at them.

WARNING: Once in the End, you won't be able to get out alive unless you manage to defeat the Ender Dragon.

Before you even think about attacking the dragon, you need to destroy the ender crystals that sit on top of the obsidian pillars since these crystals will heal it.

Shoot them with arrows, snowballs, or eggs until they explode. If you don't have any, use ladders to climb up to the top of the pillars.

Now for the difficult part: defeating the Ender Dragon. Try shooting it with arrows and keep an eye on its health bar to check how close you are to finishing it off. **And what happens if you succeed? Well, we wouldn't want to give away the secret . . .**

TIP: You can use a bed as a weapon in the End. Place it on the ground in front of you, and when the dragon gets near enough, use it as if you want to sleep, then jump back quickly. The bed will explode in the dragon's face, damaging its health.

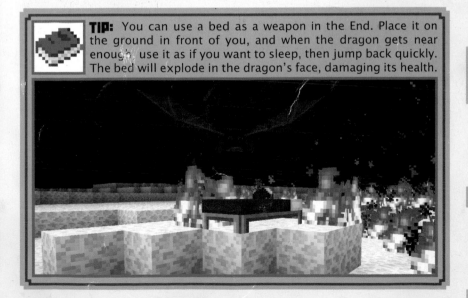

ENCHANTING

Weapons and armor can be enchanted to improve their strength and performance and to give you a real edge over your opponents. There are several ways to enchant items.

USING AN ENCHANTMENT TABLE

An enchantment table is crafted from 4 obsidian blocks, 2 diamonds, and 1 book. Craft a book from 1 piece of leather (often dropped by cows when they die) and 3 pieces of paper (made from 3 pieces of sugar cane). You won't need the leather on the Console or Pocket Editions.

PAPER RECIPE

BOOK RECIPE

ENCHANTMENT TABLE RECIPE

Access your enchantment table, then place the item you wish to enchant in the item square, and a piece of lapis lazuli in the lapis square, then choose one of the three options that appear on the right. The options are written in the standard galactic alphabet so you won't know which one you're choosing until the item is enchanted. The numbers that appear to the right of the standard galactic alphabet text tell you how many experience points you'll have to pay.

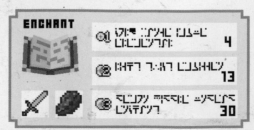

ENCHANT

48

ENCHANTING ... CONTINUED

COMBINING ITEMS ON AN ANVIL

An anvil can be used to combine enchantments from 2 items. The second item will lose its enchantment to fix the first. The items used must be the same for this to work, e.g. 2 diamond swords. Place the item to be fixed in the first anvil slot, and the other item in the second slot. The fixed item will then appear in the output slot. This will also cost you experience points.

REPAIR & NAME

Diamond Chest plate_

 +   →

Enchantment Cost: 7

 TIP: Remember, you can also rename your item when on an anvil — just type over the text in the item name box to give it a new name.

COMBINING WITH AN ENCHANTED BOOK

You can find enchanted books in chests within strongholds, dungeons, jungle temples, desert temples, mineshafts, and villages. You can also buy them with emeralds from NPC (Non-Player Character) village librarians, or make them on an enchantment table. To enchant an item, place the book in the sacrifice slot of your anvil and add the item to be enchanted.

REPAIR & NAME

Diamond Sword_

Enchantment Cost: 7

TRADING WITH A VILLAGER

Some villagers will give you enchanted items for a fee of emeralds. The items they can enchant include iron and diamond swords, axes, pickaxes, fishing rods, and chest plates.

Have a wander around your world until you come across a village — it'll look like the one on this page. You'll soon spot villagers scurrying around in the vicinity. The villagers that will trade enchanted items are the brown-robed fisherman, the black-aproned armorer, the black-aproned weaponsmith, the black-aproned toolsmith, and the white-aproned leatherworker. Just interact with a villager, and their profession will appear at the top of their trading screen.

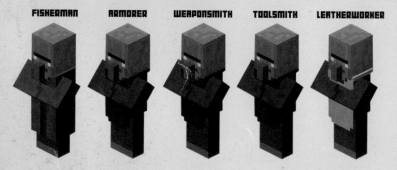

FISHERMAN　　ARMORER　　WEAPONSMITH　　TOOLSMITH　　LEATHERWORKER

You'll need to complete a few trades with the villager before the enchanted item trades will become available. When one comes up, put the requested amount of emeralds in the villager's trading slot, then the enchanted item will appear in the output square.

Just bear in mind that you won't be able to choose the enchantment yourself — the villager will let you know what option is available.

WEAPONSMITH

🪨 12 → ⚔️

Hit arrows to scroll through trade options

→

TRADING SLOTS   **OUTPUT**

DID YOU KNOW?

Receiving an enchanted item from a villager won't cost you any experience points. Awesome!

POTIONS

Potions are drinkable items that have either a positive or negative effect on a player. When used correctly, potions can really give you the upper hand in combat, so take some time to learn the basics.

BREWING STAND RECIPE

First, craft a brewing stand from a blaze rod and cobblestone. This is tricky, because blaze rods are only dropped by blazes (creatures found in or near Nether fortresses in the Nether). *Eek!* See pages 34–39 for tips on how to survive in the Nether.

CAULDRON RECIPE

Next, you'll need to craft a cauldron from 7 iron ingots.

BUCKET RECIPE

Craft a bucket, fill it with water, then use it to fill the cauldron.

GLASS BOTTLE RECIPE

Craft glass bottles from glass blocks. 3 glass blocks will give you 3 bottles.

= 3

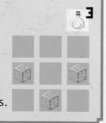

 TIP: If you're going to get serious about potions, you'll need to set yourself up with a state-of-the-art potions lab, like this one. Find a suitable spot in your home, base, or fort, and fill it with all the necessary equipment and ingredients.

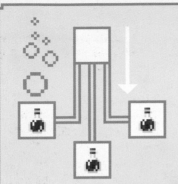

Fill 3 glass bottles with water from the cauldron and place 1 in each slot on your brewing stand.

AWKWARD POTION RECIPE

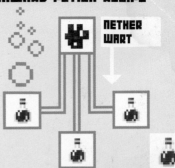

NETHER WART

3 bottles of awkward potion can be made by adding Nether wart to the top of your brewing stand. Nether wart can be found near staircases in Nether fortresses. Awkward potion doesn't do anything on its own, but when combined with others it creates useful potions. Awkward, huh?

DID YOU KNOW? Awkward potion can be used as a base potion for all helpful potions. Make sure you have a good supply of Nether wart at all times so that you're always ready to brew up a new batch.

HELPFUL POTIONS

Helpful potions have a positive or helpful effect when used. Once made, you can select a potion in your hotbar and use it to drink it. You will need 4 basic ingredients:

 Blaze powder: made from a blaze rod, dropped by blazes in the Nether

 Magma cream: dropped by magma cubes in the Nether or crafted from blaze powder and a slimeball

 Ghast tear: dropped by ghasts when killed

 Sugar: crafted from sugar cane

POTION OF STRENGTH

Made from awkward potion plus blaze powder, this potion will increase the amount of combat damage you can inflict on players or mobs.

BLAZE POWDER RECIPE

Place a blaze rod in your crafting grid to create blaze powder.

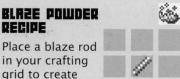

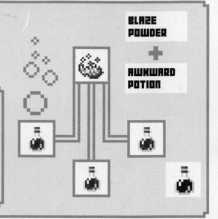

BLAZE POWDER

+

AWKWARD POTION

POTION OF HEALING

Made from awkward potion plus glistering melon, this potion will help you heal when you've been injured by restoring 4 health points per potion.

GLISTERING MELON RECIPE

A melon slice and 8 golden nuggets will make a glistering melon.

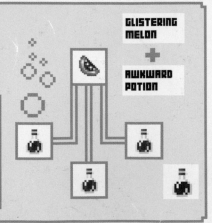

GLISTERING MELON

+

AWKWARD POTION

POTION OF SWIFTNESS

Made from awkward potion plus sugar, this potion will help you move more quickly, jump farther, and see farther.

SUGAR RECIPE

Simply add sugar cane to your crafting grid to make sugar.

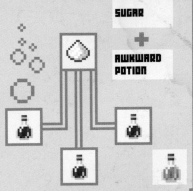

SUGAR

+

AWKWARD POTION

POTION OF INVISIBILITY

Made from awkward potion plus a golden carrot (to make potion of night vision), plus fermented spider eye (see page 60), this will make the drinker invisible.

GOLDEN CARROT RECIPE

You'll need 8 golden nuggets and 1 carrot to make a golden carrot.

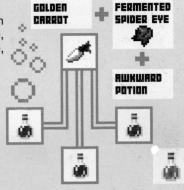

GOLDEN CARROT

+

FERMENTED SPIDER EYE

+

AWKWARD POTION

POTION OF REGENERATION

Made from awkward potion plus a ghast tear, this potion restores 18 health points over time by regenerating 1 health point per 2.5 seconds.

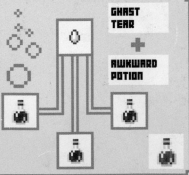

GHAST TEAR

+

AWKWARD POTION

POTION OF NIGHT VISION

Made from awkward potion plus a golden carrot, this potion will give you the ability to see in the dark by brightening everything you can see to light level 15 (daylight).

GOLDEN CARROT RECIPE

Place a carrot in your crafting grid surrounded by 8 golden nuggets.

GOLDEN CARROT

+

AWKWARD POTION

POTION OF FIRE RESISTANCE

Made from awkward potion plus magma cream, this potion will make you immune to fire, lava, and ranged blaze attacks.

MAGMA CREAM

+

AWKWARD POTION

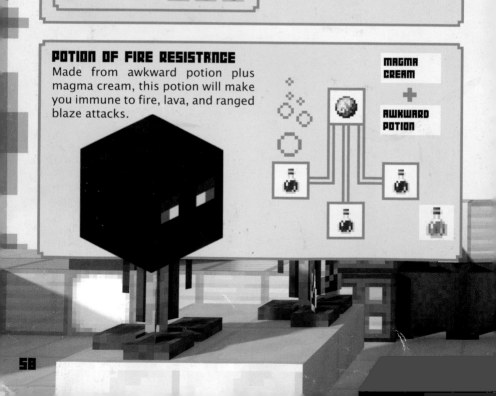

POTION OF WATER BREATHING

Made from awkward potion plus a pufferfish, this potion will allow you to breathe underwater and also help you see slightly better while you're down there.

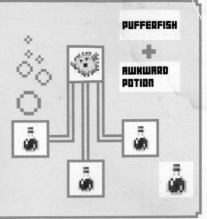

POTION OF LEAPING

Made from awkward potion plus a rabbit's foot, this potion will allow you to jump higher and reduces the fall damage you take.

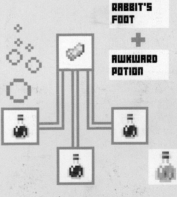

HARMFUL POTIONS

You can use spider eyes and fermented spider eyes to create harmful potions to throw at your opponents. (See splash potions on the opposite page.) Spider eyes can be obtained by killing spiders or cave spiders, and may also be dropped by witches.

FERMENTED SPIDER EYE RECIPE

1 fermented spider eye can be crafted from a spider eye, a mushroom, and sugar. Yuck. Do not mistake this for a tasty snack.

POTION OF HARMING

You can make this in two ways: potion of healing plus fermented spider eye, or potion of poison plus fermented spider eye. It will inflict 6 damage points on your opponent.

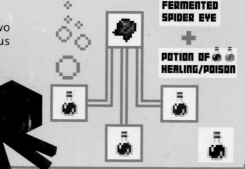

FERMENTED
SPIDER EYE
+
POTION OF
HEALING/POISON

POTION OF POISON

Made from awkward potion plus spider eye, this potion will poison the drinker for 22 seconds. The player loses 1 health point every 1.25 seconds until the poison wears off, but the effect will stop when a player only has 1 health point remaining.

SPIDER EYE
+
AWKWARD
POTION

POTION OF WEAKNESS

You can make this in two ways: potion of strength plus fermented spider eye or potion of regeneration plus fermented spider eye. This potion will reduce your opponent's melee/close-quarters attack strength by half for 1 minute 30 seconds.

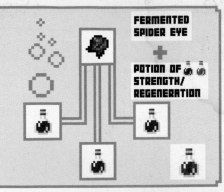

FERMENTED SPIDER EYE

+

POTION OF STRENGTH/ REGENERATION

POTION OF SLOWNESS

Made in two ways: potion of fire resistance plus fermented spider eye, or potion of swiftness plus fermented spider eye. This potion will reduce your opponent's walking ability to a crawl, and reduce the distance they can jump for 1 minute 30 seconds.

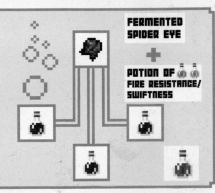

FERMENTED SPIDER EYE

+

POTION OF FIRE RESISTANCE/ SWIFTNESS

SPLASH POTIONS

A splash potion is a potion that can be thrown. You can turn any brewable potion into a splash potion simply by combining it with gunpowder. Brewing potions that have negative effects with gunpowder create splash potions that can be used as weapons against your opponents. Once brewed, place them in your hotbar and hit the Use Item button to throw them at your opponents.

POISON   WEAKNESS   SLOWNESS   HARMING

PLAYER VS PLAYER

Player versus player, or PVP, is a mode of multiplayer gameplay where you can battle against other players. You can tackle your opponents alone, or break off into teams. It's loads of fun!

ORGANIZED

Organized PVP refers to PVP that you have chosen to participate in. If you join a dedicated PVP server or organize a PVP game with your friends, you can be said to be playing organized PVP. Many organized PVP games are set in specially built arenas. These are usually constructed in Creative mode, then the host changes the game type to Survival and opens the server to other players.

UNORGANIZED

Unorganized PVP refers to occasions when you are attacked unexpectedly. Picture the scene: You're wandering happily through a forest, minding your own business, when another player hits you from behind with an enchanted diamond sword, killing you in a matter of moments. That's unorganized PVP. Talk about getting stabbed in the back!

MULTIPLAYER BY PAUL SOARES JR.

PAUL SOARES JR.: Paul is a Minecraft expert and was the first person to make Minecraft tutorials for YouTube. His debut video, "How to Survive Your First Night," aired in 2010 and he has over 1,109,900 subscribers. Check out his channel for more combat tips! **youtube.com/paulsoaresjr**

Playing Minecraft with your friends and family is great fun. You can help each other survive, team up on epic adventures, share creative builds, and pull silly pranks! The possibilities are endless and all you need is a few other players and a way to connect to each other.

To play multiplayer on the Pocket Edition, your device will need to have a Wi-Fi signal, and will need to be "visible" to other devices in the local area. Select Multiplayer, then either start a new game and wait for friends to find you, or select Join Game and search for your friends.

If you want to play in multiplayer mode on the Xbox 360 Edition, you'll need Xbox Live Gold membership. You can then play with up to 8 other people, but you won't be able to access servers set up for the PC/Mac Edition. You can also try playing in split-screen mode with 3 other players on the same Xbox.

MULTIPLAYER
FOR PC/MAC EDITION

Playing multiplayer on the PC/Mac Edition is loads of fun, as you can play with much larger groups of people. You have three options:

1. START YOUR OWN DEDICATED SERVER

SEMI-ADVANCED GEEKINESS REQUIRED

A dedicated server is a specialized Minecraft server program that runs on a computer and allows others to connect to it from just about anywhere in the world. This computer is called the host, and you need to give your Internet Address to the people you have allowed to play on it. The host computer should be fairly up-to-date to provide the best possible playing experience for everyone.

You can download the Minecraft server program for free from the official Minecraft website (minecraft.net) and follow the installation instructions provided.

2. OPEN A SINGLE-PLAYER WORLD IN LAN WORLD MODE

BASIC COMPUTER SKILLS REQUIRED

If you have more than one computer at home, you can use the Open to LAN feature (already built into Minecraft) to play with others on a single-player world. This is called a LAN (local area network) world and it's fairly simple to get one up and running. Here's the scoop:

1. Open a single-player world map and press the Escape key.

2. Click the Open to LAN button.

3. Choose the Player Settings for this session, i.e. Game Mode and Allow Cheats.

4. Click Start LAN World.

Now, at the other computers on your local network, run Minecraft, choose Multiplayer, and your LAN World should appear. Select it, hit the Join Server button, and let the games begin!

3. PLAY ON A DEDICATED ONLINE SERVER OR NETWORK

A ZOMBIE PIGMAN COULD DO IT

If you don't want to run your own server and don't mind playing with strangers, you can join an existing online server. Just click Multiplayer, Add Server, and enter the server address. That's the easy part.

The hard part is deciding which servers to add! There are thousands to choose from and each has its own set of rules, style of play, and players. Try searching an online database such as minecraftservers.net for options. Many server operators advertize on popular Minecraft forums like minecraftforum.net in order to recruit new players.

Remember, these sites aren't monitored by Mojang or Scholastic so enter at your own risk. (See page 6 for our Stay Safe Online policy.)

Holiday event on Paulsoaresjr's private family server.

PVP BATTLE CHECKLIST

Want to stay alive for as long as possible during organized PVP? Then you've got to be smart and get organized. Use this PVP checklist when preparing for battle.

TIP: Create a system for your inventory, so that all food items are stored in one area, weapons in another, potions in another, and so on. This will help you quickly transfer them to your hotbar in the middle of a battle.

Check

- Full set of armor (iron at minimum) with an enchantment — like protection or unbreaking

- At least 2 swords with enchantments like sharpness, smite, and knockback

- An enchanted bow with at least 20 arrows

- TNT

- A lava bucket

- A water bucket

- Flint and steel

- Splash potion of poison

- Splash potion of weakness

- Splash potion of harming

- Potion of invisibility

- Potion of healing

- Potion of regeneration

- Mushroom soup (see page 70)

- Steak

- Golden apples, which not only restore food points but also give you Regeneration II for 5 seconds and Absorption for 2 minutes.

When playing PVP, make sure you've stored all your valuables in a chest in your base. DO NOT take them with you, or you'll end up donating them to the player who finishes you off. Hide your chest under the floor to make it more difficult for raiders to find.

BATTLE STRATEGY

An experienced warrior knows that battle is all about strategy. It's not just about blowing people up — it's about planning your actions in advance and using your brain to gain the upper hand.

You could try running straight into the middle of a battle, hitting out at everyone and everything, but you'll be more successful if you try using these tips instead:

Craft a map as soon as you can to keep track of your location, as well as other players. Head for higher ground so you can see farther and pounce on players below you.

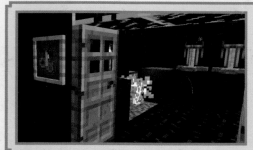

Find a suitable spot for your base and get building. Try to position it away from other players. Sky bases and underground bases are the most difficult for your opponents to locate. Build your base from the strongest substance you can lay your hands on. Obsidian is best!

Pick off your enemies one by one. This is much easier than engaging in battle with several players at once. Approach them from behind to give you the element of surprise, then use the strafing technique, which involves circling them to make it harder for them to target you.

If you can force your opponent into water their movement will be slowed, giving you an advantage.

Keep your hand empty until face-to-face with an opponent, then select your weapon. This will lull them into a false sense of security. Try to get the first hit in, so that your opponent's health points are immediately depleted.

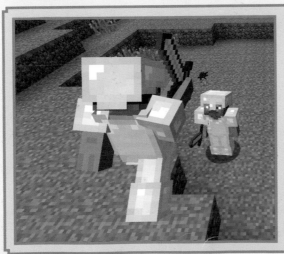

Sprint hitting, where you sprint at your enemy then hit them, enables you to knock them back farther. Try block hitting (hitting and blocking at the same time). This allows you to deal damage to your opponent while taking less in return. Also, hit your opponent while jumping to deal more damage. This is called a critical hit.

Try mushroom souping! Save a sword in the first slot of your hotbar and mushroom stew/soup in the other 8. When your health has decreased to half mid-battle, block hits while simultaneously eating your stew. This allows you to regenerate health.

Remember your potions and splash potions. A potion of invisibility can be especially helpful when you want to take your opponents by surprise. Swiftness, healing, and strength will really give you the upper hand. (Remember to take off your armor when using a potion of invisibility as it will still show up to other players.)

Place cobwebs in your enemy's path. They'll either get stuck in the cobwebs temporarily or will be forced to move around them. Either way, it'll slow them down.

When you're not looking for a fight, use the sneak function so that your name is hidden from other players and you can keep a low profile.

Always keep a few dirt blocks in your inventory. That way you can quickly build yourself a tower to stand on if there's no other way to avoid attack from other players.

FORT BATTLEGROUND

BY FYREUK

Now that you're learning the Way of the Warrior, it's time to make a battleground on which to test out your new combat skills! A fort is the perfect setting for that epic battle you've been planning.

This fort, made by FyreUK, is an impressive battleground that includes many effective features. Turn the page to see how to create some of these features.

ARROW-FILLED DISPENSERS

Have you spotted the dispensers on the second level of the tower? They're filled with arrows, and they face the entrances. Pressure plates behind allow you to activate them. Now you can fire arrows at attacking players while remaining under cover. (See page 11 for the dispenser recipe.)

SOUL SAND TRAP

Add soul sand to slow players down in open areas (this can be found in the Nether). You can place it sporadically, giving skilled players a chance to jump through it, or you can create a solid layer, forcing players to travel around it.

LAVA MOAT

A traditional castle moat would be filled with water, but where's the fun in that? Fill it with lava instead and your opponents won't stand a chance. You'll need a few buckets of lava to fill a moat of this size. Keep placing the lava until the moat fills up.

CACTI MOAT

Alternatively, fill your moat with cacti, placed as closely together as possible. You could create a hidden entrance to the fort as a reward for any players who manage to weave through.

 TIP: Be careful when using lava if you have a wooden drawbridge or walls — you do not want to be known as The Player Who Burned Down Their Own Fort. Always keep a water bucket in your hotbar for emergencies.

LONG DROP TRAP

BY CNB MINECRAFT

This trap is invisible and virtually impossible to escape from! What looks like an innocent iron door with pressure plates is actually a trap that can send the player falling as far as the bedrock layer.

CONSTRUCTION MATERIALS

CNB MINECRAFT: Nick Farwell, aka CNB Minecraft, is a redstone wizard. He can build everything from digital clocks to mob traps.

1

You'll need a regular doorway for this trap. Once finished, it should consist of a single door with a pressure plate on either side, but don't place the pressure plates yet — as you're about to dig a very deep hole!

2

Dig your pit directly in front of the door, at least 20 blocks deep. Remember the Number One Rule: Never dig straight down. Dig a 2x1 hole so you can see what you're digging into while standing on the other block.

3

Clear a 4x2x3 block space to the side of the door for the redstone circuit that will power the trap. At the top of the cleared area, place a single sticky piston facing in toward the pit. Repeat at the bottom and place a block in front of each piston.

4

Make sure the block in front of the top piston is the same as the rest of the ground so that it blends in. Place a blue wool block between 2 sticky pistons. Place a redstone torch on the left side of the blue wool block, then place a regular block above the torch and a single piece of redstone dust below it. The redstone torch will power both pistons so they are pushed out.

5

Add a single regular piston facing the opposite way to the other 2, on the right-hand side of the blue wool block. Place another piece of redstone dust behind the regular piston.

6 Fill in the rest of the pit, then cover up the top with your wall and place your pressure plates on either side of the door. The only part of the trap now visible at ground level is a single side of the top piston. In most cases the doorway will be part of a wall, so it will be covered up completely. The next person who tries to enter is going to get a shock, and a very long drop . . .

X-ᴘʟᴏᴅɪɴɢ Tʀᴇᴇ Tʀᴀᴘ

BY CNB MINECRAFT

This simple, classic trap is great fun for playing tricks on your friends on multiplayer servers. The masterstroke is that it relies merely on other players' fundamental need to gather wood. Genius.

The trap works by triggering TNT when a player attempts to harvest the bottom of a tree trunk. It's up to you how much TNT you use, but the 12 blocks shown here are more than enough to cause some serious damage!

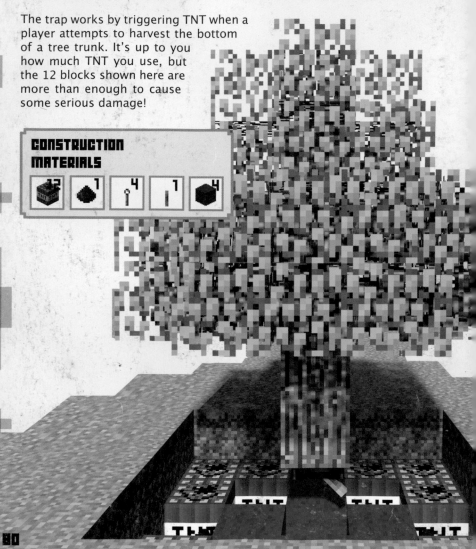

CONSTRUCTION MATERIALS

12	1	4	1	4

1

Choose a tree. Any type will work, but this example uses an oak tree. Pick a tree that is likely to be chopped down, e.g. one near another player's base.

2

Dig out an area under the tree for the TNT and the activation circuit. It will need to be 2 blocks deep, 5 wide, and 5 long, with the tree trunk positioned centrally.

3

Remove the bottom tree trunk block and place a single piece of redstone dust directly below the tree, then surround it with blue wool blocks as shown. Place a lever on the underside of the next trunk block, then flip it to the on position. The lever will provide power for the redstone dust.

4

Place redstone torches on the outer side of each wool block. These will activate the TNT when the lever is knocked off the trunk.

5

Now for the fun part — let's add the TNT! This build has 3 blocks of TNT in each corner of the pit.

6

Finally, cover the whole pit with dirt blocks (or any block that blends in with the terrain) to hide it.

7

Now all you have to do is wait for another player to undertake some tree-chopping!

TNT CANNON

This large cannon is powered by TNT and also fires TNT blocks. It causes epic levels of destruction and is especially effective if you want to blow up an approaching enemy.

CONSTRUCTION MATERIALS

1

Build a U-shape of light-green wool 6 blocks long and 3 wide, leaving a 1-block space at the back. Place redstone dust on top of each block to create a wire.

2

Starting at the front, place 4 light-green wool blocks in the center of the U-shape but raised 1 block higher. This will eventually be the water bed. Now add 1 red and 1 light-green block to the back of the cannon as shown. Place a redstone torch on top of the red wool and redstone dust on top of the light-green wool.

TnT CannOn
. . . CONTINUED

3

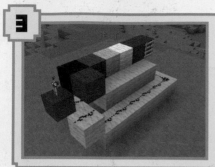

Build an L-shape of red, gray, white, and black wool, positioned a block higher than the red wool with the redstone torch attached to it. Position a ladder on the inside of the red wool at the top of the L-shape. Since ladders occupy an entire block this will act as a rest point for the TNT projectiles and will stop the water from spilling out.

4

Add a single stone slab to the end of the L-shape as shown. Aim for the top half of the red wool when placing the slab. Now add 4 dispensers opposite the longest side of the L-shape, facing in toward the water bed. These will dispense TNT into the cannon.

5

Lay redstone dust along the stone slab and the dispensers (PC/Mac users, remember to hold Shift). Place a red wool block above the redstone torch. Place 5 repeaters along the L-shape as shown, all facing toward the front of the cannon and set to 4 ticks. Using a water bucket, add a single water source block to the back of the water bed — the water will flow forward.

Add a dispenser to the top of the wool block with the ladder attached, facing in toward the water bed. Now add 2 stone slabs as shown. This will leave you with a single block of air in front of the projectile dispenser.

7

Fill all 5 dispensers with TNT and add 4 range selector buttons along the side of the cannon. Pressing the button on the white block will allow you to fire TNT the farthest, and the button on the black block will fire it the shortest distance. Have fun experimenting with range!

HOW TO BUILD
AN EPIC BASE

Your base should be as secure as possible to keep you and your possessions safe. But if you want it to be truly epic, you'll need to build something that looks intimidating enough to send your enemies running for the hills. Follow these tips to create a seriously epic base!

LOCATION
Position your base on high ground, not at the bottom of a hill. This will give you an advantage over approaching enemies, since you'll be able to see them coming. It also prevents them taking you by surprise from above.

MATERIALS
Build your base out of Nether brick. This tells your enemies that you've survived the Nether long enough to collect a lot of resources, so they might think twice about taking you on. Also, Nether brick is immune to fire, making it a good choice for a combat zone.

FLAMING NETHERRACK
Use netherrack to create floating blocks of fire at each side of the entrance. This is another great intimidation tactic — you've been to the Nether AND you like fire? Clearly, you're not to be messed with.

LAVA

Use lava wherever you can. To create streams running down the side of your base, place 4 blocks of Nether brick in a cross shape, then use a lava bucket to place lava in the center. This will create an infinite source of lava.

SECURITY

Use iron bars instead of glass for windows. They're more difficult to destroy than glass, and you'll still be able to see your enemies coming. Iron bars are technically solid blocks, so arrows can't pass through the gaps — which means you can stand behind them safely.

IRON BAR RECIPE

16

16 iron bars can be crafted from 6 iron ingots.

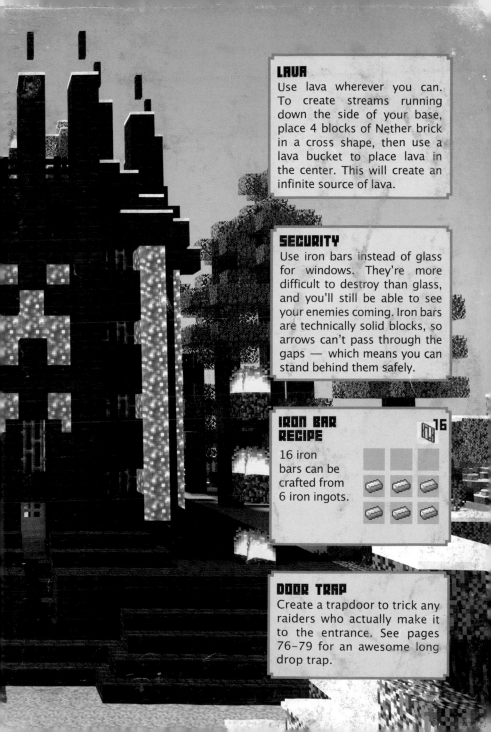

DOOR TRAP

Create a trapdoor to trick any raiders who actually make it to the entrance. See pages 76–79 for an awesome long drop trap.

RAIDING A BASE

Raiding an enemy base is a lot of fun. It provides you with more resources, and also reduces your opponents' capabilities, making them less of a threat. Here's how to do it right.

TIMING

Attack at night. When raiding an enemy base, the darkness is your friend.

RECON

Observe the area before you attack. See who's there and how to use the terrain to your advantage.

TAG TEAM

Recruit a friend to help you — two players are better than one.

TOOLS

Take the strongest tool you can. An enchanted diamond pickaxe is ideal, as it will allow you to mine tough blocks like obsidian the quickest. And remember to take spares.

YOUR ENEMY'S ENEMY

If there are any creepers around, lure them toward the base. They might just help you blow up the outer wall, free of charge.

SPLASH POTIONS
Take splash potions to use against your opponents in case they emerge.

HEALTH
Bring food to replenish your health and hunger bars.

TESTING YOUR SKILLS ON A
CUSTOM MAP BY FYREUK

Now that you've mastered the art of combat, it's time to pick up your sword, put on your helmet, and find out if you're the best warrior Minecraft has ever seen! And we've got the perfect map for you.

This is Remnant — one of FyreUK's custom Survival Games maps. Survival Games aren't just about battling one another, they're also about surviving the landscape. Within the Remnant map you'll find small villages, temples, and hidden areas containing chests filled with useful items. Your goal is to collect these items, battle the other players on the map, and win.

CHESTS
Finding chests quickly and grabbing the useful items will give you an advantage over other players.

CRAFTING RECIPES
Remember your crafting recipes, particularly the sword, bow, arrows, and armor recipes. A bow and arrows can be particularly useful on a large map as you'll be able to take out your enemies from a distance.

SNEAKING
Use the sneak function to crouch and hide your name from other nearby players (your name appears over your head in multiplayer and can be seen through blocks).

VALUABLE ITEMS

When playing the Remnant map, you won't have to run far from the start point to find valuable items. The temple in the center has multiple hidden pathways and a complex, mazelike hallway system inside, and many a treasure can be found there.

CORRIDORS

Be wary of small enclosed spaces like corridors, as you may find yourself cornered with no way out. A lot of early battles happen in small spaces.

PC/Mac users: Want to try the Remnant map for yourself? You can download it from minecraft.egmont.co.uk

Check out PlanetMinecraft (**www.planetminecraft.com**) for more downloadable custom maps.

(See page 6 for our Stay Safe Online policy.)

ACHIEVEMENT

inecraft takes note of your achievements when you're playing the PC/Mac Edition or the Console Edition. Here are some key combat achievements to aim for.

PC/MAC EDITION:

TIME TO STRIKE!
Use planks and sticks to make a sword.

MONSTER HUNTER
Attack and destroy a monster.

SNIPER DUEL
Kill a skeleton or wither skeleton with an arrow from more than 164 feet.

WE NEED TO GO DEEPER
Build a portal to the Nether.

RETURN TO SENDER
Destroy a ghast with a fireball.

THE END?
Locate the End.

THE END
Defeat the Ender Dragon.

OVERKILL
Deal 8 hearts of damage in a single hit.

THE BEGINNING?
Spawn the wither.

THE BEGINNING
Kill the wither.

CONSOLE EDITION:

TIME TO STRIKE!
Use planks and sticks to make a sword.

MONSTER HUNTER
Attack and destroy a monster.

INTO THE NETHER
Build a portal to the Nether.

USEFUL LINKS

Congratulations! You've made it to the end of the Minecraft Combat Handbook, which means you're now a fearsome warrior. Your enemies had better beware!

Check out this list of useful websites. They'll really help you take your Minecrafting to the next level.

Official Minecraft website:
https://minecraft.net

Official Mojang website:
https://mojang.com

The Minecraft wiki:
www.minecraftwiki.net

The official Facebook page:
www.facebook.com/minecraft

Mojang Team's YouTube channel:
www.youtube.com/teammojang

The official Minecraft Twitter page:
https://twitter.com/mojang

Jeb's official Twitter page:
https://twitter.com/jeb_

Some other Minecraft sites, not monitored by Mojang or Scholastic. Enter at your own risk!

Detailed server information:
minecraftservers.net

Texture packs:
www.minecrafttexturepacks.com

Minecraft on Reddit:
www.reddit.com/r/Minecraft/

Paul Soares Jr.'s YouTube channel:
www.youtube.com/paulsoaresjr

FyreUK's YouTube channel:
www.youtube.com/fyreuk

(See page 6 for our Stay Safe Online policy.)